NATIONAL GEOGRAPHIC

T0045522

This Is an Island

Belle Perez

This is an **island**.
There is water
all around the island.

There is a waterfall on the island.

There is a **mountain** on the island.

There is a forest on the island.

There is a beach on the island.
There is water
all around the island.

Picture Glossary

beach

mountain

forest

waterfall

island